ICONS

SEASIDE STYLE

SEASIDE

Living on the Beach   Interiors

STYLE

Details

Diane Dorrans Saeks

EDITOR **Angelika Taschen**

TASCHEN

KÖLN LONDON LOS ANGELES MADRID PARIS TOKYO

Cover: Sunbathing on the coast of Los Vilos, Chile
Umschlag: Sonnenbaden bei Los Vilos an der chilenischen Küste
Couverture: Bain de soleil à Los Vilos sur la côte du chilienne
Photo: Guy Wenborne

Pages 2 and 3: Sailing in the Aegean Sea, Greece
Seite 2 und 3: Segeln in der Ägäis in Griechenland
Pages 2 et 3: Voguer sur la mer Egée, Grèce
Photo: Paul Ryan/International Interiors

Page 9: On Catherine Feric's terrace, St. Barthélemy, Guadeloupe
Seite 9: Auf der Terrasse von Catherine Feric, St. Barthélemy, Guadeloupe
Page 9: Sur la terrasse de Catherine Feric, St. Barthélemy, Guadeloupe
Photo: Jean-Pierre Godeaut & Philippe Seulliet/Inside

Also available from TASCHEN:

Seaside Interiors
Trilingual edition, 304 pages, 425 ills.
3–8228–6414–5
3–8228–6159–6 (edition with French cover)

To stay informed about upcoming TASCHEN titles, please request our magazine at
www.taschen.com or write to TASCHEN, Hohenzollernring 53, D–50672 Cologne,
Germany, Fax: +49-221-254919. We will be happy to send you a free copy
of our magazine which is filled with information about all of our books.

© 2002 TASCHEN GmbH
Hohenzollernring 53, D-50672 Köln
www.taschen.com

Edited by Angelika Taschen, Cologne
Cover design by Angelika Taschen, Claudia Frey, Cologne
Text edited by Ursula Fethke, Cologne, Petra Frese, Dortmund
Lithography by Horst Neuzner, Cologne

Printed in Italy
ISBN 3–8228–1204–8

CONTENTS INHALT SOMMAIRE

I spent my childhood summers in New Zealand at the beach, diving into churning waves, floating on limpid aquamarine water, and racing along the sea-slick sands, swallowing great gulps of air that tasted of sea urchins and salt and seaweed. Snorkeling for hours, I glimpsed garden-green underwater worlds of sunlight flashing and refracting on limpet shells, blanched coral branches and skittering crabs. Schools of silvery fish darted among the rocks and disappeared. Zigzagging across Diamond Harbour in the South Island in an old sailboat, I dreamed of explorers crossing oceans and seas, their hopes filling the sails and buoying their brave ships. The coast has always been a point of departure, offering up all the inspiration in the world. Golden days on the shore spun by

BLUE HORIZONS
Diane Dorrans Saeks

Während meiner Kindheit in Neuseeland verbrachte ich die Sommermonate am Strand. Ich tauchte ein in stampfende Wellen, ließ mich treiben auf glasklarem, aquamarinblauem Wasser, rannte an feucht-glitschigen Stränden entlang und sog gierig die Meerluft ein, die nach Seeigeln und Salz und Algen schmeckte. Bei stundenlangen Schnorchelausflügen entdeckte ich die grasgrün gefärbte Unterwasserwelt. Da brach sich blitzendes Sonnenlicht an den Gehäusen von Napfschnecken und ließ Korallen und hin und her flitzende Krabben erbleichen. Silbrig glänzende Fischschwärme tauchten pfeilschnell zwischen Felsen auf und verschwanden wieder. Auf einem Segeltörn über Diamond Harbour auf der Südinsel träumte ich in einem alten Segelboot von Entdeckern, wie sie Meere und Ozeane erkundeten, wie ihre Hoffnungen die Segel blähten und ihre Schiffe über das Wasser

J'ai passé tous les étés de mon enfance sur la plage en Nouvelle-Zélande, plongeant dans les vagues, faisant la planche sur une eau limpide aigue-marine ou courant sur le sable humide, inspirant de grandes bouffées d'air frais qui sentait bon le sel, les oursins et les algues. Pendant des heures, armée de mon masque et de mon tuba, j'observais des jardins sous-marins où les rayons du soleil faisaient scintiller les berniques, les branches de corail et les crabes fuyants. Des bancs de poissons argentés fusaient entre les rochers avant de disparaître. Zigzaguant dans un vieux voilier à travers Diamond Harbour, sur l'île du Sud, je rêvais d'explorateurs traversant les océans, leurs espoirs gonflant leurs voiles et poussant en avant leurs vaisseaux intrépides. La côte a toujours été un point de départ, offrant toute l'inspiration du monde. Les jours dorés se succédaient as we gathered triangular white pipi shells in hand-woven flax baskets, built labyrinthian sandcastles decorated with seagrass and shells, and spent the last pearlescent hours of the day lying in the warm sand dunes watching the tide and feeling the cool, salty air licking sunburnt shoulders. Even when it was dark, we never wanted to go inside. The coast is an infinite world. The sea and salt air and sunshine engage all the senses, and heighten a sense of well-being. Freed of noise and complication, the seaside mind can float free, listening for the soprano sounds of the wind, the reassuring screech and squawk of seagulls. Escaping the city, sunstruck sailors follow the stars over the horizon to discover islands beyond the band of blue. In search of the perfect beach, I've headed

trieben. Die Küste war immer schon ein Symbol für Aufbruch. Sie bot alle Inspirationen, die die Welt zu geben hatte. Goldene Ta-ge am Strand vergingen wie im Flug, während wir dreieckige weiße »pipi shells« in handgeflochtenen Flachskörben sammelten, labyrinthische Sandburgen bauten, diese mit Strandhafer und Muscheln dekorierten und die letzten perlmuttschimmernden Stunden des Tages in den warmen Dünen verbrachten, wo wir das Nahen der Flut beobachteten und fühlten, wie die kühle, salzige Luft an unseren sonnenverbrannten Schultern leckte. Nie wollten wir hineingehen, selbst nachdem es schon dunkel geworden war. Die Küste ist eine unendliche Welt. Meer, salzige Luft und Sonne nehmen sämtliche Sinne gefangen. Befreit vom Lärm und allen Komplikationen kann der Geist sich am Meer unbeschwert bewegen, dem Sopran des Windes nachhängen

tandis que nous recueillions des coquillages dans des paniers en lin tressés à la main, construisions des châteaux de sable labyrinthiques ornés d'algues et de coquillages, et passions les dernières heures cuivrées de la journée couchés dans les dunes, à contempler la marée et à sentir l'air frais et iodé lécher nos épaules brûlées par le soleil. Même une fois la nuit tombée, nous ne voulions pas rentrer à la maison. La côte est un monde sans fin. La mer, l'air salé et le soleil titillent tous les sens et renforcent le sentiment de bien-être. Loin du bruit et des complications, l'esprit envoûté par la mer peut errer librement, écouter le chant de soprano du vent, les cris rassurants des mouettes. Fuyant la ville, les marins ivres de soleil suivent les étoiles au-dessus de la ligne d'horizon pour aller découvrir des îles de l'autre côté du grand bleu. En quête de la plage parfaite,

to the shore in many other parts of the world since those glory days of picnics and tide pools and seagulls. I've beach-combed in Sri Lanka, Salvador de Bahia, the Côte d'Azur, Big Sur, Mendocino, Mykonos, Zihuatanejo in Mexico, Rio de Janeiro, Long Island, Goa, Costa Careyes, Bar Harbor on the coast of Maine, Penzance in Cornwall, Bondi Beach near Sydney, Palm Beach, New Zealand's Kare Kare, Majorca, and Camber Sands on the south-east coast of England. I've got shells, sand in my sandals, and pockets full of memories. We would like to take you with this book on a journey to some of the most beautiful and purest places on the globe. Skies are cerulean blue. Follow us as we set sail for distant, dreamy shores.

und dem beruhigenden Kreischen der Seemöwen. Seit jenen wunderbaren Tagen voller Picknicks und Tidenlöchern und Seemöwen bin ich auf der Suche nach dem perfekten Strand. Ich durchkämmte die Strände auf Sri Lanka und bei Salvador de Bahia, an der Côte d'Azur und in Big Sur, bei Mendocino, auf Mykonos, im mexikanischen Zihuatanejo, in Rio de Janeiro, auf Long Island und Goa, Bar Harbor an der Küste von Maine, Penzance in Cornwall, Bondi Beach bei Sydney, Palm Beach, Costa Careyes, dem neuseeländischen Kare Kare, auf Mallorca und in Camber Sands an der Südostküste von England. Von dort brachte ich Muscheln, Sand in meinen Sandalen und wunderbare Erinnerungen mit. Wir wollen Sie mit diesem Buch an einige der schönsten und ursprünglichsten Orte dieser Welt entführen. Folgen Sie uns, wenn wir die Segel setzen und Kurs nehmen auf weit entfernt liegende Traumstrände.

j'ai sillonné les rivages de bien des coins de la planète depuis ces jours heureux de pique-niques, de barbotage et de mouettes. J'ai passé au peigne fin les plages du Sri Lanka, de Salvador de Bahia, de la Côte d'Azur, de Big Sur en Californie, de Mendocino, de Mykonos, de Zihuatanejo au Mexique, de Rio de Janeiro, de Long Island, de Goa, de la Costa Careyes, de Bar Harbor sur la côte du Maine, de Penzance en Cornouailles, de Bondi Beach près de Sydney, de Palm Beach, de Kare Kare en Nouvelle-Zélande, de Majorque et de Camber Sands dans le sud-est de l'Angleterre. J'ai des coquillages et du sable dans mes sandales et des souvenirs plein les poches. Avec ce livre nous aimerions vous emmener visiter certains des endroits les plus beaux et les plus purs du monde entier. Le ciel est d'un bleu céruléen. Suivez-nous maintenant tandis que nous mettons le cap sur des rivages lointains et enchanteurs.

"I mentioned before that I had a great mind to see the whole island, and that I had travelled up the brook, and so on to where I built my bower, and where I had an opening quite to the sea on the other side of the island."

Daniel Defoe, Robinson Crusoe (1719)

»Wie schon erwähnt, hatte ich große Lust, die ganze Insel zu besichtigen, war auch schon den Bach hinaufgewandert und weiter bis zu dem Ort, wo ich meine Laube gebaut und von wo ich einen Ausblick gegen die See auf der anderen Seite der Küste hatte.«

Daniel Defoe, Robinson Crusoe (1719)

«J'ai déjà mentionné que j'avais grande envie de visiter toute l'île, et j'étais déjà monté en longeant le ruisseau et au-delà jusqu'à l'endroit où j'avais construit ma tonnelle et où j'avais une vue sur la mer de l'autre côté de l'île.»

Daniel Defoe, Robinson Crusoé (1719)

LIVING ON THE BEACH

Leben am Strand   Vivre à la plage

12/13 At Knokke-Heist Beach in Flanders. *Am Strand von Knokke-Heist in Flandern.* La plage de Knokke-Heist dans les Flandres. *Photo: Paul Ryan/International Interiors*

14/15 Christopher Crooks and Mandy Coakley's house in England. *Das Haus von Christopher Crooks und Mandy Coakley in England.* La maison de Christopher Crooks et Mandy Coakley. *Photo: Andrew Wood/Interior Archive*

16/17 Johan Brauner's 200 year-old cottage on Gotland. *Das 200 Jahre alte Haus von Johan Brauner auf Gotland.* La maison bicentenaire de Johan Brauner à Gotland. *Photo: Ingalill Snitt/Inside*

18/19 Low tide on the Ile de Noirmoutier in France. *Ebbe am Strand von Noirmoutier in Frankreich.* Marée basse sur l'île de Noirmoutier en France. *Photo: Ivan Terestchenko/Inside*

20/21 The romantic fishing port of Cadaqués on the Costa Brava. *Der romantische Fischerhafen Cadaqués an der Costa Brava.* Le port de pêche de Cadaqués sur la Costa Brava. *Photo: Andreas von Einsiedel*

22/23 Franco Menna's terrace on the Aeolian island Filicudi. *Die Terrasse von Franco Menna auf der äolischen Insel Filicudi.* La terrasse de Franco Menna sur l'île éolienne de Filicudi. *Photo: Martti Järvi/J B Visual Press*

24/25 On the terrace of Franco Menna on Filicudi. *Auf der Terrasse von Franco Menna auf Filicudi.* Sur la terrasse de Franco Menna à Filicudi. *Photo: Martti Järvi/J B Visual Press*

26/27 View from Paolo Deganello's rustic pergola on Filicudi. *Blick von Paolo Deganellos rustikaler Pergola auf Filicudi.* Vue depuis la pergola rustique de Paolo Deganello à Filicudi. *Photo: Martti Järvi/J B Visual Press*

28/29 Moroccan style at Flavio Albanese's house on Pantelleria. *Marokkanisches Ambiente in Flavio Albaneses Haus auf Pantelleria.* Style marocain chez Flavio Albanese à Pantelleria. *Photo: Michel Arnaud/Corbis Outline*

31/32 Flavio Albanese's summer residence on Pantelleria. *Flavio Albaneses Sommerresidenz auf Pantelleria.* La résidence d'été de Flavio Albanese à Pantelleria.
Photo: Michel Arnaud/Corbis Outline

32/33 The terrace of Nicolas Feuillatte's house in Tunisia. *Die Terrasse des Hauses von Nicolas Feuillatte in Tunesien.* La terrasse de la maison de Nicolas Feuillatte en Tunisie.
Photo: Deidi von Schaewen

34/35 Beautiful view from an Arabic house in Tangier. *Der fantastische Blick von einem arabischen Haus in Tanger.* Vue superbe sur l'océan depuis une maison arabe à Tanger.
Photo: Deidi von Schaewen

36/37 Inside Gian Paolo Barbieri's house in the Seychelles. *Im Haus von Gian Paolo Barbieri auf den Seychellen.* Dans la maison de Gian Paolo Barbieri aux Seychelles.
Photo: Gian Paolo Barbieri

38/39 Pool at Gian Paolo Barbieri's retreat in the Seychelles. *Der Pool von Gian Paolo Barbieris Haus auf den Seychellen.* La picine de la maison de Gian Paolo Barbieri aux Seychelles.
Photo: Gian Paolo Barbieri

40/41 Tiny harbor in rough and romantic Maine. *Kleiner Hafen in der wildromantischen Natur von Maine.* Petit port dans la nature sauvage et romantique du Maine.
Photo: Tria Giovan

42/43 Brightly painted cottages at Cape Cod, Massachusetts. *Fröhlich bemalte Hütten auf Cape Cod in Massachusetts.* Des maisons aux couleurs gaies à Cape Cod, Massachusetts.
Photo: Andrew Garn

44/45 Breathtaking view from the Staudes' house in Big Sur. *Atemberaubender Blick vom Haus der Staudes in Big Sur.* Vue époustouflante depuis la maison des Staude à Big Sur.
Photo: Todd Eberle

46/47 Gian Franco Brignone's open living room in Mexico. *Gian Franco Brignones offener Wohnraum in Mexiko.* Le séjour ouvert de Gian Franco Brignone au Mexique.
Photo: Sofia Brignone www.careyes.com.mx

48/49 Terrace at Gian Franco Brignone's Mexican house. *Terrasse an Gian Franco Brignones Haus in Mexiko.* Terrasse de la maison mexicaine de Gian Franco Brignone. *Photo: Sofia Brignone www.careyes.com.mx*

50/51 Endless view of the Caribbean Sea from the island of Nevis. *Endloser Blick von der Insel Nevis auf das karibische Meer.* Vue infinie sur la mer des Caraïbes depuis l'île de Nevis. *Photo: Antoine Bootz*

52/53 Pool at holiday houses on Nevis designed by Studio MORSA. *Pool von Ferienhäusern auf Nevis, entworfen von Studio MORSA.* Piscine à Nevis, conçue par le Studio MORSA. *Photo: Antoine Bootz*

54/55 Sunbathing on the coast of Los Vilos, Chile. *Sonnenbaden bei Los Vilos an der chilenischen Küste.* Bain de soleil à Los Vilos sur la côte du chilienne. *Photo: Guy Wenborne*

56/57 The Reinés family on the beach of Trancoso, Brazil. *Die Familie Reinés am Strand von Trancoso in Brasilien.* La famille Reinés sur la plage de Trancoso au Brésil. *Photo: Tuca Reinés*

58/59 Alan Faena's blue and white beach house in Uruguay. *Alan Faenas blauwei-ßes Strandhaus in Uruguay.* La maison de plage bleue et blanche d'Alan Faena en Uruguay. *Photo: Reto Guntli*

60/61 Pia and Andrès Ferreyra's beach house in Uruguay. *Das Strandhaus von Pia and Andrès Ferreyra in Uruguay.* La maison de plage de Pia et Andrès Ferreyra en Uruguay. *Photo: Mirjam Bleeker & Frank Visser/Taverne Agency*

62/63 Tom Kurth's tropical resort on Hana Iti, Tahiti. *Tom Kurths tropisches Ferienparadies auf Hana Iti, Tahiti.* L'hôtel tropical de Tom Kurth sur l'île de Hana Iti à Tahiti. *Photo: Guy Hervais & Bibi Gex*

64/65 Exotic bungalows at Tom Kurth's resort in Tahiti. *Exotische Bungalows in Tom Kurths Hotelanlage in Tahiti.* Des bungalows exotiques dans le complexe hotelier de Tom Kurth à Tahiti. *Photo: Guy Hervais & Bibi Gex*

66/67 A Tahitian-style house in Tom Kurth's tropical resort. *Ein Haus im tahitianischen Stil im Tom Kurths Urlaubsparadies.* Une maison tahitienne dans l'hôtel de Tom Kurth. *Photo: Guy Hervais & Bibi Gex*

68/69 The entrance of "If" House on a beach in Sri Lanka. *Der Eingang von »If« House an einem Strand auf Sri Lanka.* L'entrée de la maison «If» sur une plage à Sri Lanka. *Photo: Deidi von Schaewen & Philippe Seulliet*

70/71 An Australian beach house designed by Larry Eastwood. *Ein australisches Strandhaus, entworfen von Larry Eastwood.* Une maison de plage en Australie, conçue par Larry Eastwood. *Photo: Simon Kenny/Belle/Arcaid*

"The house felt almost as much like a ship as a house. Placed there to ride out storms, it was built into the island as though it were a part of it; but you saw the sea from all the windows and there was good cross ventilation so that you slept cool on the hottest nights."
Ernest Hemingway, Islands in the Stream (1970)

»Das Haus glich fast eher einem Schiff als einem Haus. Es war so gebaut, dass es den Stürmen trotzen konnte, und war auf die Insel gesetzt, als wäre es ein Teil von ihr. Trotzdem gingen alle Fenster aufs Meer hinaus und auch in heißen Nächten durchwehte es eine Brise, so dass man gut schlafen konnte.«
Ernest Hemingway, Inseln im Strom (1970)

«La maison tenait presque autant d'un bateau que d'une maison. Placée là pour tenir tête aux tempêtes, elle était construite dans l'île comme si elle en faisait partie ; mais toutes les fenêtres donnaient sur la mer et l'intérieur était bien aéré, ce qui fait que l'on dormait bien au frais même pendant les nuits les plus chaudes.»
Ernest Hemingway, Iles à la dérive (1970)

INTERIORS

Interieurs Intérieurs

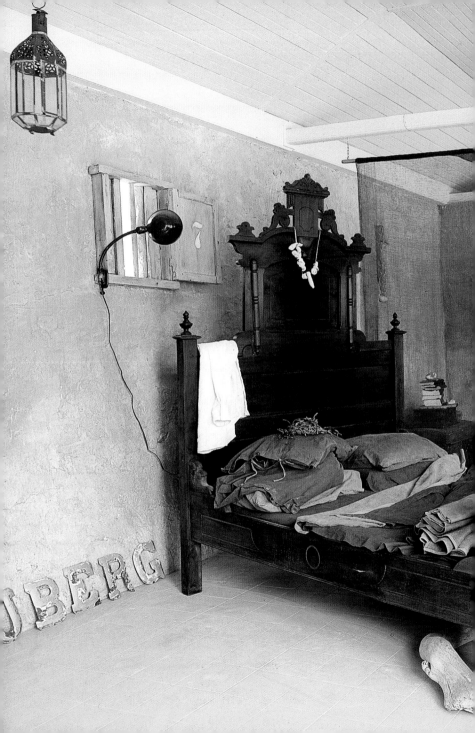

78/79 Sleeping child in Johan Brauner's house on Gotland. *Schlafendes Kind in Johan Brauners Haus auf Gotland.* Enfant endormi dans la maison de Johan Brauner à Gotland. *Photo: Ingalill Snitt/Inside*

80/81 Tami and Anders Christiansen's living room in Cadaqués. *Tami und Anders Christiansens Wohnzimmer in Cadaqués.* Le salon de Tami et Anders Christiansen à Cadaqués. *Photo: Andreas von Einsiedel*

82/83 Unpretentious and charming: inside the Christiansens' house. *Unprätentiöser Charme: im Haus der Christiansens.* Charme sans prétention: dans la maison des Christiansen. *Photo: Andreas von Einsiedel*

84/85 Bold architecture in Victor Esposito's house on Ibiza. *Kühne Architektur in Victor Espositos Haus auf Ibiza.* L'architecture hardie de la maison de Victor Esposito à Ibiza. *Photo: Sølvi Dos Santos/Inside*

86/87 The simple kitchen in Victor Esposito's house on Ibiza. *Die einfache Küche in Victor Espositos Haus auf Ibiza.* La cuisine sobre de la maison de Victor Esposito à Ibiza. *Photo: Sølvi Dos Santos/Inside*

88/89 Franco Menna's pleasantly cool terrace on Filicudi, Italy. *Franco Mennas angenehm kühle Terrasse auf Filicudi, Italien.* La terrasse fraîche de Franco Menna à Filicudi en Italie. *Photo: Martti Järvi/J B Visual Press*

90/91 The perfect place for lunch in Franco Menna's house. *Der ideale Platz für das Mittagessen in Franco Mennas Haus.* L'endroit idéal pour le déjeuner chez Franco Menna. *Photo: Martti Järvi/J B Visual Press*

92/93 Cool blue in Franco Menna's house on Filicudi. *Kühles Blau in Franco Mennas Haus auf Filicudi.* La fraîcheur du bleu dans la maison de Franco Menna à Filicudi. *Photo: Martti Järvi/J B Visual Press*

94/95 Rustic charm in Paolo Deganello's house on Filicudi. *Rustikaler Charme in Paolo Deganellos Haus auf Filicudi.* Le charme rustique dans la maison de Paolo Deganello à Filicudi. *Photo: Martti Järvi/J B Visual Press*

96/97 Flavio Albanese's summer residence on Pantelleria. *Flavio Albaneses Sommerresidenz auf Pantelleria.* La résidence d'été de Flavio Albanese à Pantelleria. *Photo: Michel Arnaud/Corbis Outline*

98/99 Albanese's study in the traditional architecture of Pantelleria. *Albaneses Arbeitszimmer im traditionellen Baustil Pantellerias.* L'architecture traditionnelle du bureau d'Albanese. *Photo: Michel Arnaud/Corbis Outline*

100/101 Flavio Albanese's colorful living room on Pantelleria. *Flavio Albaneses farbenfrohes Wohnzimmer auf Pantelleria.* Le salon bigarré de Flavio Albanese à Pantelleria. *Photo: Michel Arnaud/Corbis Outline*

102/103 Deborah French's bedroom on Mykonos. *Schlafzimmer von Deborah French auf Mykonos.* La chambre de Deborah French à Mykonos.
Photo: Paul Ryan/International Interiors

104/105 Terrace of Pedro Espirito Santo's tiny Portuguese house. *Terrasse an Pedro Espirito Santos Häuschen in Portugal.* La terrasse de la maisonette de Pedro Espirito Santo.
Photo: Lucien Kaplan/Milù Cachat

106/107 A simple shower stall in Pedro Espirito Santo's cottage. *Eine einfache Dusche in Pedro Espirito Santos Häuschen.* Un coin douche toute simple chez Pedro Espirito Santo.
Photo: Lucien Kaplan/Milù Cachat

108/109 A cool simple room in a house in Morocco. *Ein kühler, schlichter Raum in einem Haus in Marokko.* Une chambre fraîche et simple dans une maison au Maroc.
Photo: Deidi von Schaewen

110/111 Gian Paolo Barbier's living room in the Seychelles. *Das Wohnzimmer von Gian Paolo Barbieri auf den Seychellen.* Le séjour de Gian Paolo Barbieri aux Seychelles.
Photo: Gian Paolo Barbieri

112/113 In Gian Paolo Barbieri's kitchen in the Seychelles. *In Gian Paolo Barbieris Küche auf den Seychellen.* Dans la cuisine de Gian Paolo Barbieri aux Seychelles.
Photo: Gian Paolo Barbieri

114/115 Gerda and André Botha's guesthouse near Cape Town. *Gerda und André Bothas Pension in Südafrika bei Kapstadt.* La pension de Gerda et André Botha près du Cap.
Photo: Jac de Villiers/House and Leisure

116/117 In Olga Opsahl-Gee and Peter Gee's house on Cape Cod. *Im Haus von Olga Opsahl-Gee und Peter Gee auf Cape Cod.* La maison d'Olga Opsahl-Gee et Peter Gee à Cap Code.
Photo: Andrew Garn

118/119 Olga Opsahl-Gee and Peter Gee's old barn on Cape Cod. *Olga Opsahl-Gees and Peter Gees Scheune auf Cape Cod.* La grange d'Olga Opsahl-Gee et Peter Gee à Cape Cod.
Photo: Andrew Garn

120/121 Vincente Wolf's luminous living room on Long Island. *Vincente Wolfs lichterfülltes Wohnzimmer auf Long Island.* Le séjour baigné de lumière de Vincente Wolf à Long Island.
Photo: Antoine Bootz

122/123 Inside Ellen O'Neill's century-old house at Sag Harbor. *In Ellen O'Neills 100 Jahre altem Haus in Sag Harbor.* Dans la maison centenaire d'Ellen O'Neill à Sag Harbor.
Photo: Jürgen Frank/J B Visual Press

124/125 Splendid view from Carey and Andrew King's Florida home. *Herrlicher Blick aus Carey und Andrew Kings Haus in Florida.* Vue magnifique depuis la maison de Carey et Andrew King en Floride.
Photo: Tria Giovan

126/127 Donald Sterzin and Mark Campell's porch, Fire Island. *Die Veranda von Donald Sterzin und Mark Campell, Fire Island.* La véranda de Donald Sterzin et Mark Campell. *Photo: Thibault Jeanson/Inside*

128/129 Marguerite and Tony Staude's redwood house in Big Sur. *Das Redwood-Haus von Marguerite und Tony Staudes in Big Sur.* La maison en séquoia des Staude à Big Sur. *Photo: Todd Eberle*

130/131 The Staudes' house is a tribute to California's nature. *Das Haus der Staudes ist eine Hommage an Kaliforniens Natur.* La maison des Staude rend hommage à la nature. *Photo: Todd Eberle*

132/133 Holiday house created by Studio MORSA on Nevis. *Ferienhaus auf Nevis, gestaltet vom Studio MORSA.* Maison de vacances à Nevis créée par le Studio MORSA. *Photo: Antoine Bootz*

134/135 Green room in the house created by Studio MORSA on Nevis. *Grünes Zimmer im Haus des Studio MORSA auf Nevis.* Chambre verte créée par le Studio MORSA à Nevis. *Photo: Antoine Bootz*

136/137 Gian Franco Brignone's dramatic lookout terrace, Mexico. *Gian Franco Brignones dramatische Aussichtsterrasse, Mexiko.* La terrasse panoramique de Gian Franco Brignone au Mexique. *Photo: Sofia Brignone www.careyes.com.mx*

138/139 Frank Visser's shady outdoor dining room in Curaçao. *Frank Vissers schattiges Freiluft-Esszimmer in Curaçao.* La salle à manger ombragée de Frank Visser à Curaçao. *Photo: Mirjam Bleeker & Frank Visser/Taverne Agency*

140/141 Bed in Frank Visser's simple one-room hacienda in Curaçao. *Bett in Frank Vissers Einraumhacienda in Curaçao.* Lit dans une hacienda d'une seule pièce à Curaçao. *Photo: Mirjam Bleeker & Frank Visser/Taverne Agency*

142/143 Pia and Andrès Ferreyra's boat-like kitchen, Uruguay. *Die bootartige Küche von Pia und Andrès Ferreyra, Uruguay.* La cuisine-bateau de Pia et Andrès Ferreyra. *Photo: Mirjam Bleeker & Frank Visser/Taverne Agency*

144/145 In the Ferreyras' summer house at Cabo Polonio. *Im Sommerhaus der Ferreyras am Cabo Polonio.* Dans la maison d'été des Ferreyra à Cabo Polonio. *Photo: Mirjam Bleeker & Frank Visser/Taverne Agency*

146/147 A bed in a canoe in the home of the Ferreyras. *Ein Bett in einem Kanu in dem Haus der Ferreyras.* Un lit dans un canoë dans la maison des Ferreyras. *Photo: Mirjam Bleeker & Frank Visser/Taverne Agency*

148/149 Simple bed in Toti and João Calazans' house in Brazil. *Einfaches Bett in Toti und João Calazans' Haus in Brasilien.* Un lit tout simple pour Toti and João Calazans au Brésil. *Photo: Tuca Reinés & Mario de Castro*

150/151 Calazanses' cool blue and white kitchen of the in Brazil. *Die kühle blauweiße Küche der Calazans in Brasilien.* La fraîche cuisine bleue et blanche des Calazans au Brésil. *Photo: Tuca Reinés & Mario de Castro*

152/153 Alan Faena's living room in Uruguay. *Ein Farbenmeer: Alan Faenas Wohnzimmer in Uruguay.* De la couleur à profusion: le séjour d'Alan Faena en Uruguay. *Photo: Reto Guntli*

154/155 View from Cristián Boza's living room in Los Vilos, Chile. *Blick aus Cristián Bozas Wohnzimmer in Los Vilos in Chile.* Vue depuis séjour de Cristián Boza à Los Vilos au Chili. *Photo: Guy Wenborne*

156/157 The Saldañas' house in the Philippines. *Das Haus der Saldaña auf den Philippinen.* La maison des Saldaña aux Philippines. *Photo: Marie Pierre Morel & Daniel Rozensztroch/Marie Claire Maison*

158/159 A breezy Australian house created by Larry Eastwood. *Luftiges australisches Haus, entworfen von Larry Eastwood.* Maison aérée créée par Larry Eastwood en Australie. *Photo: Simon Kenny/Belle/Arcaid*

160/161 The open living room of a house in Australia. *Das offene Wohnzimmer eines Hauses in Australien.* Un séjour ouvert en Australie. *Photo: Simon Kenny/Belle/Arcaid*

162/163 The bright kitchen of an Australian beach house. *Die helle Küche in einem australischem Strandhaus.* La cuisine lumineuse d'une maison de plage australienne. *Photo: Simon Kenny/Belle/Arcaid*

"… and on a cold night he would sit in the big chair in front of the fire, reading by the lamp that stood on the heavy plank table and look up while he was reading to hear the north-wester blowing outside and the crashing of the surf and watch the great, bleached pieces of driftwood burning."

Ernest Hemingway, Islands in the Stream (1970)

» … und wenn es kalt war nachts, saß er in seinem großen Stuhl vor dem Feuer und las im Licht der Lampe, die auf dem schweren Plankentisch stand, und er sah beim Lesen auf und hörte den Nordwestwind draußen und das Krachen der Brandung und er sah zu, wie die großen, ausgebleichten Holzstücke verbrannten.«

Ernest Hemingway, Inseln im Strom (1970)

«… et quand la nuit était froide, il s'asseyait sur la grande chaise, devant le feu, lisant à la lueur de la lampe qui se trouvait sur la lourde table en bois, levant les yeux pour écouter le vent du nord-ouest souffler dehors et le bruit du ressac, et regarder brûler les gros morceaux aux couleurs défraîchies.»

Ernest Hemingway, Iles à la dérive (1970)

DETAILS

Details Détails

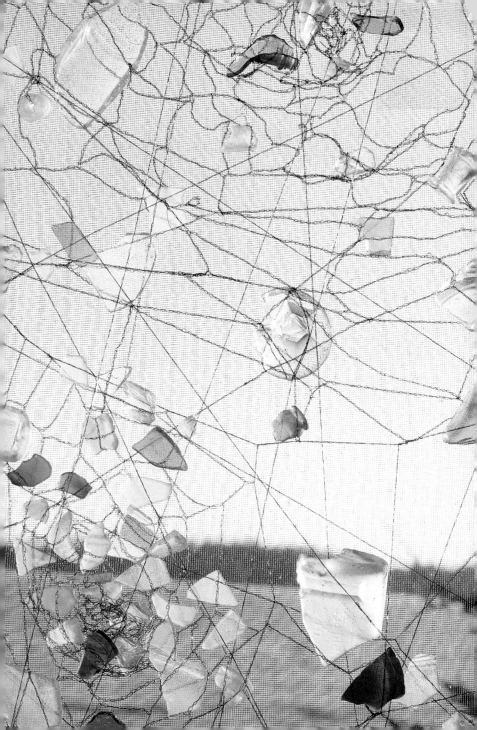

171 Bikini top at Ellen O'Neill's house on Long Island. *Bikinitop in Ellen O'Neills Haus auf Long Island.* Haut de bikini dans la maison de Ellen O'Neill à Long Island. *Photo: Jürgen Frank/ J B Visual Press*

172 Dog in an old farm house on the Ile de Noirmoutier. *Hund in einem Bauernhaus auf der Ile de Noirmoutier.* Chien dans une vieille ferme sur l'Ile de Noirmou-tier. *Photo: Ivan Terest-chenko/Inside*

173 Treasures from flea-markets on the Ile de Noirmoutier. *Flohmarktschätze auf der Ile de Noirmoutier.* Des trésors chinés aux puces sur l'Île de Noirmoutier. *Photo: Ivan Terest-chenko/Inside*

175 Living room in an old house on the Ile de Noirmoutier. *Wohnzimmer in einem alten Haus auf der Ile de Noirmou-tier.* Salle de séjour d'une vieille ferme sur l'Île de Noirmoutier. *Photo: Ivan Terest-chenko/Inside*

176 In Mandy Coakley and Christopher Crooks' house. *In Mandy Coakleys und Christopher Crooks Haus.* Dans la maison de Mandy Coakley et Christopher Crooks. *Photo: Andrew Wood/The Interior Archive*

177 The glass curtain in Judith van Amringe's Maine home. *Glasvorhang in Judith van Amringes Haus in Maine.* Rideau de verre dans la maison de Judith van Amringe dans le Maine. *Photo: Antoine Bootz*

179 In Gerda and André Botha's guesthouse near Cape Town. *In der Pension von Gerda und André Botha bei Kapstadt.* Détail de la pension de Gerda et André Botha au Cap. *Photo: Jac de Villiers/House and Leisure*

180 Entrance hall to Carla and Tuca Reinés house in Brazil. *Eingangsbereich des Hauses von Carla und Tuca Reinés in Brasilien.* Entrée de la maison de Carla et Tuca Reinés au Brésil. *Photo: Tuca Reinés*

181 Outdoor lunch at the Reinés' family retreat in Brazil. *Mittagessen im Freien am Ferienhaus der Familie Reinés in Brasilien.* Déjeuner en plein air avec la famille Reinés au Brésil. *Photo: Tuca Reinés*

182 Shower in the
house of Toti and
João Calazans in
Brazil. *Dusche in Toti
and João Calazans
Haus in Brasilien.*
Douche dans la mai-
son de Toti et João
Calazans au Brésil.
*Photo: Tuca Reinés &
Mario de Castro*

184 Inside the plea-
sant house of Toti
and João Calazans.
*In dem gemütlichen
Haus von Toti and
João Calazans.* Dans
agréable demure de
Toti et João Calazans.
*Photo: Tuca Reinés &
Mario de Castro*

185 The Calazans's
simple and functional
coat rack. *Die ein-
fache und funktionale
Garderobe Calazans.*
Le portemanteau
simple et fonctionnel
des Calazans.
*Photo: Tuca Reinés &
Mario de Castro*

187 Exotic wash
basin at Tom Kurth's
holiday resort in Tahi-
ti. *Exotisches Wasch-
becken in Tom
Kurths Ferienparadies
in Tahiti.* Cuvette
exotique dans l'hôtel
de Tom Kurth à Tahiti.
*Photo: Guy Hervais &
Bibi Gex*

188 Inside a house
built by Tom Kurth in
a banyan tree. *In
einem Haus, das
Tom Kurth in einem
Banyanbaum baute.*
L'inerieur d'une mai-
son bâtie de Tom
Kurth dans un banian.
*Photo: Guy Hervais &
Bibi Gex*

189 The kitchen of
Tom Kurth's banyan
tree house in Tahiti.
*Küche in Tom Kurths
Banyan-Baumhaus in
Tahiti.* La cuisine de
la maison de Tom
Kurth nichée dans un
banian à Tahiti.
*Photo: Guy Hervais &
Bibi Gex*

Seaside Interiors
Ed. Angelika Taschen / Diane
Dorrans Saeks / Flexi-cover,
304 pp. / € 14.99 / $ 19.99 /
£ 9.99 / ¥ 2.900

Country Interiors
Ed. Angelika Taschen / Diane
Dorrans Saeks / Flexi-cover,
304 pp. / € 14.99 / $ 19.99 /
£ 9.99 / ¥ 2.900

Tuscany Interiors
Ed. Angelika Taschen / Paolo
Rinaldi / Flexi-cover,
288 pp. / € 14.99 / $ 19.99 /
£ 9.99 / ¥ 2.900

"TASCHEN is the one to watch out for if you like
your material presented succinctly and beautifully
without gushing or extraneous filler." —*reader's comment*, amazon.com

"Buy them all and add some pleasure to your life."

All-American Ads 40ˢ
Ed. Jim Heimann

All-American Ads 50ˢ
Ed. Jim Heimann

All-American Ads 60ˢ
Ed. Jim Heimann

Angels
Gilles Néret

Architecture Now!
Ed. Philip Jodidio

Art Now
Eds. Burkhard Riemschneider,
Uta Grosenick

Berlin Style
Ed. Angelika Taschen

Chairs
Charlotte & Peter Fiell

Design of the 20ᵗʰ Century
Charlotte & Peter Fiell

Design for the 21ˢᵗ Century
Charlotte & Peter Fiell

Devils
Gilles Néret

Digital Beauties
Ed. Julius Wiedemann

Robert Doisneau
Ed. Jean-Claude Gautrand

East German Design
Ralf Ulrich / Photos: Ernst
Hedler

Eccentric Style
Ed. Angelika Taschen

Fashion
Ed. The Kyoto Costume
Institute

HR Giger
HR Giger

Graphic Design
Ed. Charlotte & Peter Fiell

Grand Tour
Harry Seidler,
Ed. Peter Gössel

Havana Style
Ed. Angelika Taschen

Homo Art
Gilles Néret

Hot Rods
Ed. Coco Shinomiya

Hula
Ed. Jim Heimann

India Bazaar
Samantha Harrison,
Bari Kumar

Industrial Design
Charlotte & Peter Fiell

Japanese Beauties
Ed. Alex Gross

Kitchen Kitsch
Ed. Jim Heimann

Krazy Kids' Food
Eds. Steve Roden,
Dan Goodsell

Las Vegas
Ed. Jim Heimann

Mexicana
Ed. Jim Heimann

Morocco Style
Ed. Angelika Taschen

**Extra/Ordinary Objects,
Vol. I**
Ed. Colors Magazine

**Extra/Ordinary Objects,
Vol. II**
Ed. Colors Magazine

Paris Style
Ed. Angelika Taschen

Penguin
Frans Lanting

Photo Icons, Vol. I
Hans-Michael Koetzle

Photo Icons, Vol. II
Hans-Michael Koetzle

20ᵗʰ Century Photography
Museum Ludwig Cologne

Pin-Ups
Ed. Burkhard Riemschneider

Provence Style
Ed. Angelika Taschen

Pussycats
Gilles Néret

Safari Style
Ed. Angelika Taschen

Seaside Style
Ed. Angelika Taschen

Albertus Seba. Butterflies
Irmgard Müsch

**Albertus Seba. Shells &
Corals**
Irmgard Müsch

Starck
Ed Mae Cooper, Pierre Doze,
Elisabeth Laville

Surfing
Ed. Jim Heimann

Sydney Style
Ed. Angelika Taschen

Tattoos
Ed. Henk Schiffmacher

Tiffany
Jacob Baal-Teshuva

Tiki Style
Sven Kirsten

Tuscany Style
Ed. Angelika Taschen

Women Artists
in the 20ᵗʰ and 21ˢᵗ Century
Ed. Uta Grosenick